ideal
school supply

FLIP-FLASH™

Math

ADDITION & SUBTRACTION FACTS

ISBN: 1-56451-351-3

©2000 Ideal School Supply • A Division of Instructional Fair Group, Inc.
A Tribune Education Company
3195 Wilson Drive NW, Grand Rapids, MI 49544 • USA
Duke Street, Wisbech, Cambs, PE13 2AE • UK
All Rights Reserved • Printed in Malaysia

ID7875

Helpful Hints for Learning the Facts

Flip and Check Say the answer to a fact, then flip the page to check. **The answer is the top number on the flip side of the page.**

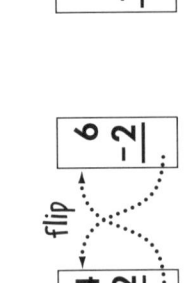

Double Your Power Learn the double-number facts. Use them to help you remember other facts.

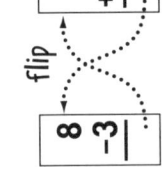

Power Up With Turnarounds Learn pairs of "turnaround" facts. If you know one, you know the other one too.

$$\begin{array}{r} 1 \\ +8 \\ \hline \end{array} \qquad \begin{array}{r} 8 \\ +1 \\ \hline \end{array} \qquad \begin{array}{r} 5 \\ +10 \\ \hline \end{array} \qquad \begin{array}{r} 10 \\ +5 \\ \hline \end{array}$$

Tackle the Hard Ones Find the facts that give you trouble. Draw a picture to help you "see" the fact in your mind.

$6+7=$

Make It a Game Make up games to help you recall the facts quickly. Play the games with your friends and family.

Addition Chart

	1	2	3	4	5	6	7	8	9	10	11	12
1	2	3	4	5	6	7	8	9	10	11	12	13
2	3	4	5	6	7	8	9	10	11	12	13	14
3	4	5	6	7	8	9	10	11	12	13	14	15
4	5	6	7	8	9	10	11	12	13	14	15	16
5	6	7	8	9	10	11	12	13	14	15	16	17
6	7	8	9	10	11	12	13	14	15	16	17	18
7	8	9	10	11	12	13	14	15	16	17	18	19
8	9	10	11	12	13	14	15	16	17	18	19	20
9	10	11	12	13	14	15	16	17	18	19	20	21
10	11	12	13	14	15	16	17	18	19	20	21	22
11	12	13	14	15	16	17	18	19	20	21	22	23
12	13	14	15	16	17	18	19	20	21	22	23	24

$$1$$
$$+1$$
_____

$$\begin{array}{r} 2 \\ -1 \\ \hline \end{array}$$

$$\begin{array}{r} 1 \\ +2 \\ \hline \end{array}$$

$$3$$
$$-2$$
$$\overline{}$$

$$\begin{array}{r} 1 \\ + 4 \\ \hline \end{array}$$

$$\begin{array}{r} 5 \\ -\,4 \\ \hline \end{array}$$

$$\begin{array}{r} 1 \\ + 6 \\ \hline \end{array}$$

$$\begin{array}{r} 7 \\ -\ 6 \\ \hline \end{array}$$

$$\begin{array}{r} 1 \\ + 8 \\ \hline \end{array}$$

$$\begin{array}{r} 9 \\ -8 \\ \hline \end{array}$$

$$1$$
$$+10$$
$$\overline{}$$

$$\begin{array}{r} 11 \\ -10 \\ \hline \end{array}$$

$$\begin{array}{r} 1 \\ +12 \\ \hline \end{array}$$

$$13$$
$$-12$$
$$\overline{}$$

$$\begin{array}{r} 2 \\ +\ 2 \\ \hline \end{array}$$

$$
\begin{array}{r}
4 \\
-2 \\
\hline
\end{array}
$$

$$\begin{array}{r} 2 \\ +3 \\ \hline \end{array}$$

$$\begin{array}{r} 5 \\ -3 \\ \hline \end{array}$$

$$\begin{array}{r} 2 \\ +5 \\ \hline \end{array}$$

$$7$$
$$-5$$
$$\overline{}$$

$$\begin{array}{r} 2 \\ +7 \\ \hline \end{array}$$

$$9$$
$$-7$$

$$\begin{array}{r} 2 \\ + 9 \\ \hline \end{array}$$

$$11$$
$$-\ 9$$

$$\begin{array}{r} 2 \\ +11 \\ \hline \end{array}$$

$$13$$
$$-11$$
$$\overline{}$$

$$3$$
$$+1$$
$$\overline{}$$

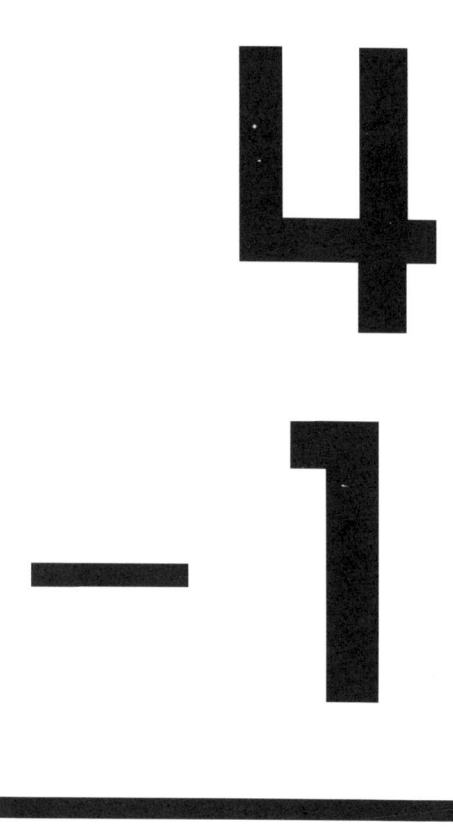

$$\begin{array}{r} 3 \\ + 3 \\ \hline \end{array}$$

$$6$$
$$-3$$
$$\overline{}$$

$$
\begin{array}{r}
3 \\
+\,4 \\
\hline
\end{array}
$$

$$\begin{array}{r} 7 \\ -4 \\ \hline \end{array}$$

$$\begin{array}{r} 3 \\ +6 \\ \hline \end{array}$$

$$9$$
$$-6$$
$$\overline{}$$

$$\begin{array}{r} 3 \\ + 8 \\ \hline \end{array}$$

11
− 8
_____

$$\begin{array}{r} 3 \\ +10 \\ \hline \end{array}$$

$$13$$
$$-10$$
$$\overline{}$$

$$\begin{array}{r} 3 \\ +12 \\ \hline \end{array}$$

$$\begin{array}{r} 15 \\ -12 \\ \hline \end{array}$$

$$\begin{array}{r} 4 \\ + 2 \\ \hline \end{array}$$

$$\begin{array}{r} 6 \\ -\ 2 \\ \hline \end{array}$$

$$\begin{array}{r} 4 \\ +\ 4 \\ \hline \end{array}$$

$$8$$
$$-4$$
$$\overline{}$$

$$
\begin{array}{r}
4 \\
+\ 5 \\
\hline
\end{array}
$$

$$9$$
$$-\ 5$$
$$\overline{}$$

$$\begin{array}{r} 4 \\ +7 \\ \hline \end{array}$$

$$11$$
$$-7$$
$$\overline{}$$

$$
\begin{array}{r}
4 \\
+\ 9 \\
\hline
\end{array}
$$

$$\begin{array}{r} 13 \\ -9 \\ \hline \end{array}$$

$$\begin{array}{r} 4 \\ +11 \\ \hline \end{array}$$

$$\begin{array}{r} 15 \\ -11 \\ \hline \end{array}$$

$$\begin{array}{r} 5 \\ +1 \\ \hline \end{array}$$

$$\begin{array}{r} 6 \\ -1 \\ \hline \end{array}$$

$$\begin{array}{r} 5 \\ +3 \\ \hline \end{array}$$

$$\begin{array}{r} 8 \\ -3 \\ \hline \end{array}$$

$$
\begin{array}{r}
5 \\
+5 \\
\hline
\end{array}
$$

$$
\begin{array}{r}
10 \\
-5 \\
\hline
\end{array}
$$

$$\begin{array}{r} 5 \\ +6 \\ \hline \end{array}$$

$$\begin{array}{r} 11 \\ -\ 6 \\ \hline \end{array}$$

$$\begin{array}{r} 5 \\ +8 \\ \hline \end{array}$$

$$13 - 8$$

$$\begin{array}{r} 5 \\ +10 \\ \hline \end{array}$$

$$\begin{array}{r} 15 \\ -10 \\ \hline \end{array}$$

$$\begin{array}{r} 5 \\ +12 \\ \hline \end{array}$$

$$\begin{array}{r} 17 \\ -12 \\ \hline \end{array}$$

$$\begin{array}{r} 6 \\ +2 \\ \hline \end{array}$$

$$8 - 2$$

$$\begin{array}{r} 6 \\ +4 \\ \hline \end{array}$$

$$\begin{array}{r} 10 \\ -\ 4 \\ \hline \end{array}$$

$$\begin{array}{r} 6 \\ +6 \\ \hline \end{array}$$

$$\begin{array}{r} 12 \\ -\ 6 \\ \hline \end{array}$$

$$\begin{array}{r} 6 \\ +7 \\ \hline \end{array}$$

$$13 - 7$$

$$\begin{array}{r} 6 \\ + 9 \\ \hline \end{array}$$

$$15$$
$$-9$$

$$\begin{array}{r} 6 \\ +11 \\ \hline \end{array}$$

17
−11
———————

$$\begin{array}{r} 7 \\ +1 \\ \hline \end{array}$$

$$\begin{array}{r} 8 \\ -1 \\ \hline \end{array}$$

$$\begin{array}{r} 7 \\ + 3 \\ \hline \end{array}$$

$$\begin{array}{r} 10 \\ -3 \\ \hline \end{array}$$

$$\begin{array}{r} 7 \\ +5 \\ \hline \end{array}$$

$$12 - 5$$

$$\begin{array}{r} 7 \\ +7 \\ \hline \end{array}$$

$$
\begin{array}{r}
14 \\
-\ 7 \\
\hline
\end{array}
$$

$$\begin{array}{r} 7 \\ +8 \\ \hline \end{array}$$

$$15$$
$$-\ 8$$
$$\overline{}$$

$$\begin{array}{r} 7 \\ +10 \\ \hline \end{array}$$

$$17$$
$$-10$$

$$\begin{array}{r} 7 \\ +12 \\ \hline \end{array}$$

$$\begin{array}{r} 19 \\ -12 \\ \hline \end{array}$$

$$\begin{array}{r} 8 \\ +2 \\ \hline \end{array}$$

$$\begin{array}{r} 10 \\ -\ 2 \\ \hline \end{array}$$

$$\begin{array}{r} 8 \\ + 4 \\ \hline \end{array}$$

$$\begin{array}{r} 12 \\ -\ 4 \\ \hline \end{array}$$

$$\begin{array}{r} 8 \\ + 6 \\ \hline \end{array}$$

$$14 - 6$$

$$\begin{array}{r} 8 \\ +\,8 \\ \hline \end{array}$$

$$\begin{array}{r} 16 \\ -8 \\ \hline \end{array}$$

$$\begin{array}{r} 8 \\ + 9 \\ \hline \end{array}$$

$$\begin{array}{r} 17 \\ -\ 9 \\ \hline \end{array}$$

$$\begin{array}{r} 8 \\ +11 \\ \hline \end{array}$$

$$\begin{array}{r} 19 \\ -11 \\ \hline \end{array}$$

$$9$$
$$+1$$
$$\overline{}$$

$$\begin{array}{r} 10 \\ -\ 1 \\ \hline \end{array}$$

$$\begin{array}{r} 9 \\ +3 \\ \hline \end{array}$$

$$\begin{array}{r} 12 \\ -3 \\ \hline \end{array}$$

$$\begin{array}{r} 9 \\ + 5 \\ \hline \end{array}$$

$$14 - 5$$

$$\begin{array}{r} 9 \\ +7 \\ \hline \end{array}$$

$$16$$
$$-\ 7$$

$$\begin{array}{r} 9 \\ + 9 \\ \hline \end{array}$$

$$18 - 9$$

$$\begin{array}{r} 9 \\ +10 \\ \hline \end{array}$$

$$\begin{array}{r} 19 \\ -10 \\ \hline \end{array}$$

$$9$$
$$+12$$
$$\overline{}$$

$$\begin{array}{r} 21 \\ -12 \\ \hline \end{array}$$

$$10$$
$$+ 2$$
$$\overline{}$$

$$12 - 2$$

$$\begin{array}{r} 10 \\ +\ 4 \\ \hline \end{array}$$

14
− 4
―――――

$$\begin{array}{r} 10 \\ +\ 6 \\ \hline \end{array}$$

$$\begin{array}{r} 16 \\ -6 \\ \hline \end{array}$$

$$\begin{array}{r} 10 \\ + \ 8 \\ \hline \end{array}$$

$$18$$
$$-\ 8$$
$$\overline{}$$

$$\begin{array}{r} 10 \\ +10 \\ \hline \end{array}$$

$$\begin{array}{r} 20 \\ -10 \\ \hline \end{array}$$

10
+11
_____

$$21 - 11$$

$$11$$
$$+ 1$$
—————————

$$\begin{array}{r} 12 \\ -\ 1 \\ \hline \end{array}$$

$$11 + 3 \over $$

$$14$$
$$-\ 3$$

$$11$$
$$+\ 5$$

$$\begin{array}{r} 16 \\ -\ 5 \\ \hline \end{array}$$

$$11$$
$$+ 7$$
$$\overline{}$$

$$\begin{array}{r} 18 \\ -7 \\ \hline \end{array}$$

$$11 + 9$$

$$\begin{array}{r} 20 \\ -9 \\ \hline \end{array}$$

$$\frac{22}{-11}$$

$$11$$
$$+12$$
$$\overline{}$$

$$
\begin{array}{r}
23 \\
-12 \\
\hline
\end{array}
$$

$$12$$
$$+ \ 2$$
$$\overline{}$$

$$14$$
$$-\ 2$$

$$12$$
$$+\ 4$$
$$\overline{}$$

$$16$$
$$-\ 4$$

$$\begin{array}{r} 12 \\ +6 \\ \hline \end{array}$$

$$\begin{array}{r} 18 \\ -6 \\ \hline \end{array}$$

$$\begin{array}{r} 12 \\ +\ 8 \\ \hline \end{array}$$

$$\begin{array}{r} 20 \\ -\ 8 \\ \hline \end{array}$$

$$\begin{array}{r} 12 \\ +10 \\ \hline \end{array}$$

$$22$$
$$-10$$
$$\overline{}$$

$$\begin{array}{r} 12 \\ +12 \\ \hline \end{array}$$

$$24$$
$$-12$$